THE FIGHT FOR WOMEN'S
SUFFRAGE

Essential Events

THE FIGHT FOR WOMEN'S

SUFFRAGE

BY MARCIA AMIDON LUSTED

Content Consultant
Stephanie A. Smith, PhD, professor,
American Studies, University of Florida

ABDO
Publishing Company

CREDITS

Published by ABDO Publishing Company, 8000 West 78th Street, Edina, Minnesota 55439. Copyright © 2012 by Abdo Consulting Group, Inc. International copyrights reserved in all countries. No part of this book may be reproduced in any form without written permission from the publisher. The Essential Library™ is a trademark and logo of ABDO Publishing Company.

Printed in the United States of America,
North Mankato, Minnesota
062011
092011

 THIS BOOK CONTAINS AT LEAST 10% RECYCLED MATERIALS.

Editor: Mari Kesselring
Copy Editor: Rebecca Rowell
Interior Design and Production: Kazuko Collins
Cover Design: Kazuko Collins

Library of Congress Cataloging-in-Publication Data
Lusted, Marcia Amidon.
  The fight for women's suffrage / by Marcia Amidon Lusted.
     p. cm. -- (Essential events)
  Includes bibliographical references and index.
  ISBN 978-1-61783-099-0
  1. Women--Suffrage--United States--History--Juvenile
literature. I. Title.
  JK1898.L87 2012
  324.6'230973--dc22

                              2011009543

TABLE OF CONTENTS

Chapter 1	Seneca Falls	6
Chapter 2	The Weaker Sex	16
Chapter 3	From Abolition to Suffrage	26
Chapter 4	Toward a Common Cause	36
Chapter 5	Growing Pains	46
Chapter 6	Coming Together	56
Chapter 7	By Whatever Means Necessary	66
Chapter 8	The Dawn of a New Era	78
Chapter 9	The Legacy of Suffrage	88
Timeline		96
Essential Facts		100
Glossary		102
Additional Resources		104
Source Notes		106
Index		110
About the Author		112

*A sign marks the location of the Seneca Falls Convention
in Seneca Falls, New York.*

SENECA FALLS

*I*n July 1848, a short advertisement ran in
the *Seneca County Courier*, the local paper for
the small town of Seneca Falls, New York. It read:

*WOMEN'S RIGHTS CONVENTION—A convention to
discuss the social, civil, and religious condition and rights of*

women, will be held in the Wesleyan Chapel, at Seneca Falls, New York, on Wednesday and Thursday, the 19th and 20th of July, current; commencing at 10 o'clock A.M. During the first day the meeting will be exclusively for women, who are earnestly invited to attend. The public generally are invited to be present on the second day, when Lucretia Mott, of Philadelphia, and other ladies and gentlemen, will address the convention.[1]

Although short, this advertisement and the convention it announced would go down in history as the first step toward women's suffrage in the United States. Ironically, the idea for holding a convention about women's rights had started out as conversation over tea in one woman's kitchen. Five women had gathered there, friends or relations of each other: Martha Coffin Wright, her sister Lucretia Mott, Elizabeth Cady Stanton, Jane Hunt, and Mary Ann M'Clintock. It was M'Clintock's house. Stanton and Mott had met and become friends in London, England. When Mott came to see her sister Martha Wright in Seneca Falls, she was also able to visit Stanton, whose family had recently moved there from Boston, Massachusetts. What began as a social visit became a pivotal moment in history.

They Wrote the Book

One of the lasting contributions Stanton, Susan B. Anthony, Ida Husted Harper, and Matilda Joslin Gage made to the suffrage movement was to write a chronicle of the struggle. *A History of Woman Suffrage* is six volumes long. Begun in 1876, it took 14 years to complete just the first half. The work is a complete history of the suffrage movement in the United States. It includes reminiscences from the pioneers of suffrage, which was especially important for the writers to capture as many of them grew older and died. The other three volumes were completed in 1922.

A Discussion and an Idea

The five women had discussed the recent passage of the New York Married Women's Property Rights Act of 1848. At the time, many married women did not have the right to own property, keep their own wages, sign contracts, or bring a lawsuit. The Property Act of 1848 was a first step to granting women some of these rights. It allowed a woman to keep property that was hers before her marriage. She also retained the right to any inheritances made to her during her marriage. It was not a comprehensive act that gave women all the rights that men already had, but it was a start.

As the women discussed the act, Stanton argued that perhaps it was time for all of women's rights to be made public. Stanton felt that only women themselves could accomplish this. Before the end of their tea party, the five women had decided to hold a women's convention. The convention would discuss women's conditions and what needed to be done to improve women's rights. The seed for the Seneca Falls Convention was planted.

Stanton was a good writer, and it became her job to draw up a declaration of sentiments that would form the framework for the convention. She used the US Declaration of Independence as a guide and listed 18 separate points. She called these points "injuries and usurpations," that men had committed against women.[2] The Declaration of Sentiments read, in part,

> The history of mankind is a history of repeated injuries and usurpations on the part of man toward woman, having in direct object the establishment of an absolute tyranny over her. To prove this, let facts be submitted to a candid world.
>
> He has never permitted her to exercise her inalienable right to the elective franchise. He has compelled her to submit to laws, in the formation of which she had no voice. He has withheld from her rights which are given to the most ignorant and degraded men—both natives and foreigners. Having deprived her of this first right of a citizen, the elective franchise, thereby leaving her without representation in the halls of legislation, he has oppressed her on all sides. He has

made her, if married, in the eye of the law, civilly dead. He has taken from her all right in property, even to the wages she earns.[3]

Stanton also wrote 11 resolutions, which pointed out that women had the right to be equal to men in all areas. The ninth resolution includes the revolutionary idea that it was women's duty to gain the right to vote for their gender. This idea shocked even Mott:

> *Elizabeth Cady Stanton afterwards recalled that a shocked Lucretia Mott exclaimed, "Why, Lizzie, thee will make us ridiculous." Stanton stood firm. "But I persisted, for I saw clearly that the power to make laws was the right through which all other rights could be secured."*[4]

The Seneca Falls Convention

On the morning of July 19, the organizers of the convention arrived at the church in Seneca Falls

---

The Yellow Rose

The yellow rose was a symbol of the suffrage movement since its beginnings, most likely because of the yellow rose bush Stanton's mother planted in her daughter's garden, which still blooms today. During the struggle in Tennessee to gain the last vote needed for ratification of the amendment that would give women the vote, suffrage supporters wore yellow roses, while the antisuffragists wore red roses.

DECLARATION OF SENTIMENTS

When, in the course of human events,
it becomes necessary for one portion of the family of man
to assume among the people of the earth
a position different from that which they have hitherto occupied,
but one to which the laws of nature
and of nature's God entitle them,
a decent respect to the opinions of mankind require:
that they should declare the causes
that impel them to such a course.

We hold these truths to be self-evident:
that all men and women are created equal;
that they are endowed by their Creator

Stanton's Declaration of Sentiments is on display in Seneca Falls.

where the convention would take place. However, they discovered the church locked and no key to be found. The convention, despite the large number of people who had already gathered, was in danger of failing before it even began. Finally, Stanton had one of her nephews crawl through an open window to unlock the church from inside.

None of the women expected a large turnout for their convention. Only one small advertisement had been placed in a local paper. They also thought the time of year, when farmers were busy with their crops, might limit the number of attendees. However, nearly 300 people gathered. Many of them were women, but men also attended. The advertisement had limited first-day

Why Not Let Women Vote?

It is hard to imagine a good reason why women should be barred from voting. When the suffrage movement began, there were many established ideas of a woman's role in society. Many worried that if women could vote, it would be the first step to a complete collapse of those societal roles. Men feared that women who supported suffrage would neglect their families and their household duties and that society itself would have to change completely. Others believed women were physically, emotionally, and intellectually inferior to men. They argued that women were not strong enough to withstand the rigors of using their brains, which were not developed enough to make good political decisions. They also argued that women were ruled by their emotions rather than their intellect, so women would vote according to their feelings, not according to the issues.

Even in the early days of suffrage, women were already proving that they could attend college and become doctors and ministers and lawyers without any effect on their health. Suffrage did not have to mean neglecting their families. In fact, it would give women more power to help their families by voting on issues that were vital to child and family health and safety.

attendance to women only, but the organizers decided to let the men remain. It was a wise decision, for it set a precedent that suffrage was a man's issue as well.

At the conference, some of the women felt shy or inadequate about speaking in front of so many listeners. No one really had any experience in proper parliamentary procedure for running meetings. They decided to use some of the men present to help run the meeting itself. Mott, who had done more public speaking than anyone there, stated the objectives of the convention. Mary Ann M'Clintock and her sister Elizabeth read speeches.

The most important part of the convention was to debate the Declaration of Sentiments. By the end of the two days of meeting, all but the ninth resolution—the one about women's right to vote—had

What Is in a Name?

The terms *suffragist* and *suffragette* are often used interchangeably, but they do not mean the same thing. The word *suffragette* is British. A London newspaper introduced the term, using it to belittle and make fun of the women involved in the British suffrage movement. The word *suffragist* is American and simply describes anyone involved in the suffrage movement, male or female.

passed unanimously. The ninth resolution passed, after much debate, with a very small majority of votes. The Declaration of Sentiments was signed by 100 participants: 68 women and 32 men. Of those who attended the Seneca Falls Convention, only one, Charlotte Woodward, would live to see women get to vote in 1920. She was 19 years old at the time of the convention.

The first step had been taken. The Seneca Falls Convention of 1848 was the first time women gathered and stated their dissatisfaction with their place in society and their lack of rights. Though the press and church and government leaders would ridicule the convention, those involved knew it was the beginning of a very long and important fight. No one knew then if they would succeed, but looking back at the oppression of women in the generations before them, they knew it was worth fighting for.

Stanton, with her daughter Harriot, in 1856

*Women helped the American colonies gain independence from England.
However, they were not given the same rights as men
when the new country was formed.*

THE WEAKER SEX

or the first women living in the new
North American colonies, the English
laws and customs they brought from their homeland
defined their place in society. English law at the time
stated that a woman's husband was her master. He

protected her rights, so she needed no formal legal status of her own. This included establishing the man—the head of the household—as the only one who could vote.

But women's rights—or lack of rights—went beyond the question of voting. Because of religious teachings of the Bible, which most colonial settlers followed devoutly, women were considered inferior to men. The Old Testament of the Bible claims that God says of women, "Your desire shall be for your husband, and he shall rule over you."[1] People who believed women were incapable of being voting members of society would use this argument repeatedly.

COLONIAL NORTH AMERICA

Women in colonial North America were not only without voting rights but most other rights as well. Married women could not own property. If a woman owned

Adam and Eve

The argument most frequently used against allowing women to vote—or to have many other rights—is the Christian story of Adam and Eve. According to the Bible, Adam and Eve lived in the Garden of Eden, which provided everything they might possibly need. The only stipulation God made about living there was that they should never eat from the Tree of Knowledge in the garden. However, a serpent convinced Eve to take fruit from the tree, which she and Adam both ate. God expelled both from the garden, and they were made to live more difficult lives. Many men used this story to support the theory that women were a weaker and inferior sex because Eve was first to take fruit from the forbidden tree.

Anne Hutchinson

There were women in colonial America who held positions of respect despite the restrictions of society. Anne Hutchinson came to Massachusetts in 1634 with her husband and eventually gave birth to 15 children. She was adept at preaching and held church services in her home. A newcomer to Boston commented that Hutchinson "preaches better Gospell than any of your black-coates that have been at the [university]."[2] Hutchinson attracted many followers but angered Puritan church officials because she claimed church followers did not need to go through them to gain salvation. Instead, Hutchinson preached that each person could have an individual relationship with God. She was eventually banished to Rhode Island and later moved to New York, where she and some of her children were killed during a retaliatory Native American raid.

property—goods or land—before she married, it became her husband's property. Any wages she earned also went to her husband. If a couple divorced, the husband received custody of the children. Yet, if her husband died, a woman was liable for the taxes on his property, even though she had no voice in how that tax money was used because she could not vote. American colonists eventually rebelled against England, their colonizer, because they were being taxed without a voice in the government. But women were in the same unrepresented situation even after the American Revolution (1775–1783).

In addition to having almost no legal rights, women were limited in other ways. Most women and girls did not receive education outside of the home, especially at the college level. They did not have many opportunities for employment either. They were expected to stay at home and care for their children. The one place where women could perform any other sort of role was in church. But they were usually expected to give way to men when it came to anything important and not to voice their opinions.

But as America gained its independence and began the process of forming its own government, there were already some women speaking up for the rights of their gender. Abigail Adams, wife of future president John Adams, wrote a letter to her husband as he attended the Continental Congress in March 1776. In the letter, she offered advice as he helped to write laws for the new country:

> *In the new Code of Laws which I suppose it will be necessary for you to make, I desire you would Remember the Ladies, and be more generous and favorable to them than your ancestors. Do not put such unlimited power in the hands of the Husbands. Remember all men would be Tyrants if they could. If particular care and attention are not paid to the ladies, we are determined to foment a rebellion and will not hold ourselves bound to obey any laws in which we have no voice or representation.[3]*

Abigail Adams's voice was bold for her time and place. Unfortunately, her husband replied, "As to your extraordinary code of laws, I cannot but laugh."[4] John Adams went on to oppose many measures that would have enabled more people to vote. He explained his reasoning,

> *It is dangerous to open so fruitful a source of controversy and altercation as would be opened by attempting to alter the qualifications of voters. There will be no end of it. New claims will arise; women will demand the vote.*[5]

Across the Ocean

While American women saw little improvement in their situation as their country was formed, women across the ocean in England were already pointing out gender inequalities. In 1792, English author Mary Wollstonecraft published the book *A Vindication of the Rights of Women*. While it does not specifically address suffrage, it was highly influential for some women

The Quakers

One group of women in early America who enjoyed more freedom and rights than most were members of the Quaker religion. The Religious Society of Friends, which is the formal name for the Quaker sect, promotes equality between the sexes and allows women to lead worship services and contribute their voices to community affairs. The religion teaches that every person possesses the Inner Light of the Divine Spirit, whether male or female. Quakers are also reformers, and they were some of the first people in the United States to actively oppose slavery. Many of the women who were important in launching the suffrage movement were, or had been, Quakers.

Abigail Adams hoped that her husband, John Adams, would help improve women's rights.

who would become part of the suffrage movement. Wollstonecraft asserts that men and women shared the same nature and capability to develop their abilities but women were treated as subordinates. Because of this treatment, women could not develop at the same pace intellectually as men. Wollstonecraft notes the basic concepts of equality for women. She describes how they were being denied opportunities for education and intellectual accomplishments. These concepts would become part of the feminist movement.

Wollstonecraft's words inspired women in England and the United States to start thinking about their own rights. In the United States, the old restrictions on who could vote were being changed for some people. Previously, only

New Jersey, 1797

Despite women's lack of rights and place in society in the 1700s, there was actually one state in the new country that briefly allowed women the right to vote. In New Jersey, before 1790, the voting laws granted "all free inhabitants" the right to vote.[6] Although this could be interpreted to include women, few people actually believed that "all" also meant women. But in 1790, New Jersey's legislature amended its voting laws, inserting the phrase "he or she" when referring to voters.[7] Now, it was unmistakable that women were being included in the state's voters.

The new law did not make much of an impact until 1797, however, when a group of women from Elizabethtown, New Jersey, decided to oppose the election of legislative candidate John Condit. Powerful men backed Condit, but the women's votes nearly unseated him. After the election, politicians began talking about repealing women's right to vote. Newspaper editors began publishing editorials that ridiculed and tried to intimidate women voters to keep them from voting in the future. The editorials portrayed women voters as being easily swayed by others' opinions or bullied by their husbands into voting a certain way. As a result, New Jersey women lost their right to vote in 1807. Condit sponsored the repeal.

men who owned property could vote. But by 1850, this requirement had been abolished. Some states attempted to limit voting to taxpayers, but this restriction became rare. As the number of people who did not own property increased, it became necessary to allow those without property to vote. Otherwise, too large a population would be unable to vote, which went against the concepts of liberty and equality that had become common for free men in the United States. In addition, the growth of political parties helped ease voting restrictions because these groups wanted to be able to draw more voters to their party.

There were still many classes of people who could not vote, however, including women and enslaved African Americans. In some places, free blacks and Native Americans were also barred from voting. But as more people were allowed to vote, it

Mary Wollstonecraft

Wollstonecraft, whose *A Vindication of the Rights of Women* would inspire so many suffragists, was born in England in 1759. At the age of 19, she was forced to earn her own living and established a school with her sister, Eliza. That experience led her to write her first book, *Thoughts on the Education of Daughters*. Soon after, Wollstonecraft decided to make her living from writing. In addition to *A Vindication of the Rights of Women*, she also wrote *Maria, Or the Wrongs of Woman*. She died after giving birth to a daughter, Mary, in 1797. Mary married poet Percy Bysshe Shelley and wrote *Frankenstein*. Wollstonecraft is remembered for helping women to achieve a better life and opening their eyes to their lack of rights.

became harder to exclude other groups. Soon, more changes would take place in US society that would increase women's desire to be contributing, voting citizens of their country. ⌐

Mary Wollstonecraft

*Temperance reformers prayed outside saloons
as a form of protest against alcohol.*

From Abolition to
Suffrage

In the 1800s, the United States
experienced many types of religious and
reform movements. One of the biggest religious
movements was the Second Great Awakening (the
first having taken place in the 1700s). One of the

basic ideas behind the Second Great Awakening was that an individual's salvation did not rest only with God. People could bring about their own salvation by accepting God into their lives, trying to live without sin, and making up for past sins. An individual could perform good deeds to increase his or her chances of reaching heaven.

As a result of the Second Great Awakening, religious meetings and revivals were held all over the country. People began to see that they had the power to create change in society as well as in their own lives. Women were especially drawn to the new movement and these large gatherings. The new attitude about individual choices and power would inspire the women who eventually began to fight for women's suffrage. Their increasing involvement in all aspects of religion gave women a new opportunity to assert themselves. It also gave them the chance to play a larger role outside of the home. As Nancy F. Cott explains in her book *The Bonds of Womanhood*,

> *Religious identity allowed women to assert themselves, both in private and in public ways. It enabled them to rely on an authority beyond the world of men. . . . No other avenue of self-expression besides religion at once offered women social*

approbation, the encouragement of male leaders (ministers), and, most important, the community of their peers.[1]

First Reforms

But before suffrage could take the stage as a reform movement, two other causes occupied women. Fighting for these causes would essentially help women build the skills and community necessary for their own fight for voting rights. Temperance and abolition of slavery in the South drew many women to their cause. Abolition in particular, with its stress on the basic human rights of freedom for black slaves, would naturally lead to suffrage, as women fought for their own rights as humans.

The leaders of the abolitionist movement were men. However, a large number of women also worked for the movement, finding

The Grimké Sisters

Two of the first women to defy the conventions of society and speak out were Angelina and Sarah Grimké. They were born into a slaveholding family in South Carolina, but both women hated slavery. They became Quakers and ardent abolitionists. They were also among the first women to do things women were not supposed to do, such as travel alone, publish antislavery books and essays, speak in churches, and go on lecture tours. Angelina became the first woman to speak before a legislative hearing in Massachusetts in 1838. She told her sister, "We abolition women are turning the world upside down."[2]

Abolitionist Mott attended the World Anti-Slavery Convention in London, England.

themselves in public roles for the first time. Abolitionism taught many women the basics of organization and political activism. At the time, it was considered improper for women to speak out in public, especially to a mixed audience of men and women. As women campaigned for abolitionism, they had to learn how to speak in public and present their viewpoints in a way that would further their cause. Many people still felt it was wrong and even unnatural for women to behave this way. Despite disapproval, women flocked to the abolitionist movement.

A Defining Moment

In June 1840, the World Anti-Slavery Convention was held in London. Several female delegates from the United States attended, including Mott and Stanton. At that time, a split had developed within the abolitionist societies over whether women should be allowed to hold official roles. This controversy preceded the women to London. There, male delegates argued over whether the women should attend the convention at all. Stanton

Abby Kelley's Appointment

In 1840, William Lloyd Garrison, one of the country's most prominent antislavery activists, appointed Abby Kelley to the business committee of the American Anti-Slavery Society. This was the first time a woman had been given an official position in an abolitionist organization. Her appointment created a major conflict within the society since many men opposed having women in any kind of leadership position. This controversy would reach London well before the 1840 World Anti-Slavery Convention and result in the barring of women from active involvement in that convention.

commented on the arguments, saying that "the excitement and vehemence of protest and denunciation could not have been greater."[3] The ultimate outcome was that women were barred from involvement in the convention. They were relegated to a separate section, screened by a curtain, and unable to speak or vote.

However, their exclusion from the World Anti-Slavery Convention would result in Stanton and Mott forming a friendship. This friendship would lead to the tea party in Seneca Falls and the first meeting of the US suffrage movement eight years later.

SENECA FALLS AND BEYOND

The success of the Seneca Falls Convention led to another meeting in Rochester, New York, just two days later, on July 22, 1848. This was because the Seneca Falls meeting adjourned with the decision that the

Violence

Because so many men—and even some women—were opposed to women's active involvement in the abolition movement and, often, the abolition movement in general, violence often occurred. In 1835, during a meeting of the Boston Female Anti-Slavery Society, protestors broke into the meeting and forced the women there to flee for their safety. During a meeting of the Anti-Slavery Convention of American Women in Philadelphia in 1838, protestors chased the women out of the meeting halls and set fire to it.

attendees needed more time to discuss their goals. As Stanton later wrote,

For those who do not yet understand the real objects of our recent Conventions at Rochester and Seneca Falls, I would state that we did not meet to discuss fashions, customs, or dress, the rights or duties of man, nor the propriety of the sexes changing positions, but simply our own inalienable rights.[4]

The Rochester convention adjourned with several more formal resolutions. One called for resolving unequal

Francis Parkman

In 1884, Francis Parkman, a US historian and writer, published a booklet called *Some of the Reasons against Woman Suffrage*. In it, he gives several arguments as to why women should not be allowed to vote. Parkman's essay begins with this statement:

Everybody knows that the physical and mental constitution of a woman is more delicate than in the other sex; and, we may add, the relations between mind and body are more intimate and subtle.[5]

Parkman goes on to list his arguments against allowing women to vote. These include that suffrage was cruel because of the health risks to women, since the turmoil of fighting for suffrage would cause nervous exhaustion. Parkman believed if women could vote and increase their power, then unhappy marriages would increase and the divorce rate would double. He also felt popular government would be endangered if "the most impulsive and excitable half of humanity had an equal voice in the making of laws."[6] He claimed that female politicians would use their feminine charms to bring about the downfall of powerful politicians. Parkman also thought that most women were against suffrage and that suffrage itself threatened the permanent relationships between the sexes as assigned to them by God.

economic conditions, such as laws that prevented married women from owning and inheriting property. Another condemned the government's ability to levy taxes against working women even though they were not allowed a voice in the government that taxed them. Again, the most controversial resolution was that women should be allowed to vote.

The resolutions passed in Seneca Falls and Rochester had no legal standing at all. The leaders of the newborn suffrage movement wanted to simply attract attention to their cause. They received plenty of coverage in newspapers across the country, most of it negative. The *Philadelphia Public Ledger and Daily Transcript* went so far as to claim, "A woman is a nobody. A wife is everything."[7]

But despite the negative reactions to their first two conventions, the suffrage pioneers had set a new movement in motion. Any publicity,

Bloomers

The standard outfit for women in the mid-1800s was anything but comfortable. Corsets forced women's figures into unnaturally thin shapes and layers of full petticoats and long skirts with hoops hampered their movements. This style of dress was uncomfortable and unhealthy. By the 1850s, a few of the most radical US women began adopting a new outfit known as the Bloomer outfit or just bloomers. The new style was created by, and named for, abolitionist and temperance activist Amelia Bloomer. Bloomers consisted of a pair of wide, voluminous pants worn under a knee-length skirt. Many suffrage leaders, including Stanton, Anthony, and Stone, would adopt the bloomer outfit. However, many later stopped wearing bloomers because of the derision they experienced when wearing them, which made it a "physical comfort but a mental crucifixion," according to Anthony.[8]

whether it was good or bad, helped their cause by bringing more attention to it. In the coming years, more women would join the cause.

*Although bloomers offered women an alternative to heavy skirts,
most felt awkward wearing them in public.*

Horace Greeley was a strong supporter of suffragists.

TOWARD
A COMMON CAUSE

The meetings at Seneca Falls and Rochester in 1848 had brought much-needed publicity to the suffrage movement. Despite the mostly negative press, there were some voices of support for women's right to vote. Horace Greeley, editor of the *New York Tribune*, would become a supporter of suffrage for 20 years. He wrote that women's rights meetings were simply "the assertion of a natural right and as such must be conceded."[1]

SPREADING THE WORD

Two more conventions took place in 1850, one in Salem, Ohio, and the other in Worcester, Massachusetts. The Ohio convention brought the suffrage issue farther west and attracted more women to the cause. Younger women especially, who had moved west for new opportunities and were more open to new ideas, were interested in the cause. Ohio was also the home of Oberlin College, which was the nation's first college to admit both women and blacks. Lucy Stone, who became a leader in the suffrage movement, had graduated from Oberlin in 1847.

At the Salem convention, more resolutions were adopted. The

Lucy Stone

Lucy Stone would become one of the most famous names of the suffrage movement. She was a very unusual woman for her time. She was already involved in suffrage when she married Henry Blackwell, an abolitionist, in 1855. The couple shocked the public by drafting a legal document that protected Stone from being Blackwell's property—copies were distributed to the press. Stone shocked people even more by keeping her maiden name. For many years afterward, women who kept their maiden names were known as "Lucy Stoners."

women also wrote a petition for the upcoming Ohio Constitutional Convention. In it, they reminded the male lawmakers that women had no rights and were subject to the decisions of men without any voice or legal protection. The women decided that "if the fundamental laws of the State were to be revised and amended, it was a fitting time for them to ask to be recognized."[2] The women at the Salem convention signed the memorial. By the time it was presented to the Ohio Constitutional Convention, it held thousands of signatures. However, convention attendees disregarded the petition and the discussions of the petition were dropped from the convention's proceedings.

Suffrage Goes National

With successful turnouts at the conventions in New York and Ohio, leaders of the suffrage movement decided to hold a larger gathering. The First National Women's Rights Convention was held in Worcester, Massachusetts, in October 1850. Organizers chose Worcester for its central location. The convention brought together the people who would form the foundation of the suffrage movement for the rest of the century.

Many attendees at the Worcester convention were activists for both suffrage and abolition. They provided strength for the suffrage cause and continued to educate women in how to be political activists. Unfortunately, at times, abolition and suffrage were almost in competition with each other. An example of this is illustrated in the story of Sojourner Truth.

Truth was an African American born into slavery. As a child, she had been owned by a family that spoke only Dutch. When she was sold to other families, Truth was often beaten because she did not understand English. Eventually, she moved to the North, became free, and learned English. She made money traveling and lecturing about her life as a slave. Truth was listed as an attendee at the Worcester convention in 1850. However, it was not until a women's rights convention

Indiana

The state of Indiana also held a constitutional convention in 1850. Though there was no organized women's movement in the state at that time, the cause of women's rights was argued by Robert Dale Owen, a feminist supporter. His daughter would write, years later, of the convention, "It is incredible that men in their sane minds should argue day after day that if women were allowed to control their own property, it would 'ruin the home' and 'open wide the door to . . . debauchery.'"[3]

Owen did not succeed in gaining any constitutional rights for women. However, he did spark the creation of a suffrage organization in Indiana.

Truth became a major voice for women's suffrage in the mid-1800s.

in Akron, Ohio, in 1851 that she was invited to
speak. As she approached the podium, many of the
people present were afraid that if she spoke, the

convention would be seen as an abolition meeting. Frances Dana Gage, who wrote about the Akron convention, recalled women expressing concern:

Don't let her speak, Mrs. Gage, it will ruin us. Every newspaper in the land will have our cause mixed up with abolition . . . and we shall be utterly denounced.[4]

But Truth was allowed to speak. Her "Ain't I a Woman" speech would become one of the most famous suffrage speeches:

That man over there says that women need to be helped into carriages, and lifted over ditches, and to have the best place everywhere. Nobody ever helps me into carriages, or over mud-puddles, or gives me any best place! And ain't I a woman? Look at me! Look at my arm! I have ploughed and planted, and gathered into barns, and no man could head me! And ain't I a woman? I could work as much and eat as much as a man—when I could get it—and bear the lash as well! And ain't I a woman? . . . If the first woman God ever made was strong enough to turn the world upside down all alone, these women together ought to be able to turn it back, and get it right side up again! And now they is asking to do it, the men better let them.[5]

Truth's speech pointed out that abolition and suffrage could work together. Truth became a suffrage celebrity because she immediately understood that women's rights and abolition were linked. She also asserted that women's rights were not trivial compared to the rights of slaves.

Meanwhile, more women became active in the suffrage movement. Susan B. Anthony had been working for temperance when she became a suffragist in 1852. Around this time Anthony met Stanton. The two would become prominent voices in the fight for suffrage.

THE MOB CONVENTION

In 1853, New York City hosted a world's fair. The fair

Hannah Tracy

One of the women who attended the 1850 convention in Akron, Ohio, was Hannah Tracy. She had had a difficult life. Her father had forbidden her from attending Oberlin College. Instead, she married and had three children. She was pregnant with the third child when her husband died of pneumonia while being held captive by proslavery men because he was helping slaves escape. Tracy then moved to the city of Oberlin to attend the college and also ran a boardinghouse to support herself and her children. She wrote a book of feminist theory. *Woman As She Was, Is, and Should Be* was published in 1846.

After graduating from Oberlin, Tracy became the principal of a new high school in Columbus, an impressive job for a woman. Despite the risk to her job, she attended the Akron convention. She was an example of the network of support and sisterhood that was being constructed slowly, through conventions and other suffrage meetings. Women could draw on the real-world experiences of other women who also knew what it was like to be deprived of their rights and freedom.

provided an opportunity for many groups to hold meetings, including temperance advocates, abolitionists, and suffragists. A large suffrage meeting was planned at the Broadway Tabernacle. Even with a 25¢ admission fee, all 3,000 seats were sold out. However, the conservative newspapers in New York had been inciting discontent among men who felt threatened by women taking more prominent roles in various causes. As the meeting unfolded, a mob of men disputed the speeches by stamping, hissing, and yelling. Despite the noise, the meeting's speakers still attempted to make their speeches. Finally, Truth once again took the stage:

Susan B. Anthony

Anthony started out as a temperance activist but became one of the most famous names of the suffrage movement. She joined the suffrage movement after she was refused the right to speak at antialcohol meetings because of her gender. She became a close colleague of Stanton. The women worked well together because Stanton had a way with words and could write well, while Anthony excelled at organization and public speaking. Stanton once said of the two of them, "I forged the thunderbolts and she fired them."[6]

I know that it feels a kind o' hissin' and ticklin' like to see a colored woman get up and tell you about things, and Woman's Rights. We have all been thrown down so low that nobody thought we'd ever get up again; but we have been long enough trodden now; we will come up again, and now I am here. But we'll have our rights; see if we don't; and you can't stop us from them; see if you can. You may hiss as much as you like, but it is comin'.[7]

The mob failed. Though the disruptions continued, they actually strengthened the women's cause because so many people disapproved of the way the mob was acting. The men's behavior made more people sympathetic to the suffrage cause.

As the 1850s drew to a close, women, including Stanton and Anthony, continued to hold conventions to publicize their cause. However, the movement would soon be put on hold by an event that threatened the very unity of the United States.

Susan B. Anthony

*Some women worked as nurses for soldiers
during the American Civil War.*

GROWING PAINS

s the 1850s became the 1860s, the
suffrage movement could claim little
real progress after 12 years. When petitions were
brought before state governments seeking voting
and other rights for women, they were almost always

defeated. There were few signs that suffrage was receiving any serious attention nationwide.

Then in 1861, the United States went to war with itself over the issue of slavery. The suffrage movement was put on hold as the American Civil War (1861–1865) was waged. Since many suffragists were abolitionists, most of them sided with the Union. Some suffrage leaders realized any changes resulting from the Civil War might increase opportunities for women as well.

During the war, women on both sides helped in their communities. Some women nursed soldiers on the battlefield. Others organized medical care and assembled supplies for the armies. Still others filled jobs in factories and offices and ran their family farms while the men were away at war.

Now Is the Hour

When the war ended, women felt they should be granted the right to vote as a reward for their help during the war. But controversy arose over whether voting rights for former slaves were more important than voting rights for women. Frederick Douglass, a former slave and an abolition leader, insisted that voting rights for blacks needed to come first:

I do not see how anyone can pretend that there is the same urgency in giving the ballot to woman as to the negro. With us, the matter is a question of life and death. . . . When women, because they are women, are hunted down . . . when they are dragged from their houses and hung upon lamp-posts; When their children are torn from their arms . . . when they are objects of insult and outrage at every turn . . . then they will have an urgency to obtain the ballot equal to our own.[1]

Stanton countered this by saying, "NOW'S THE HOUR—Not the 'negro's hour' alone, but everybody's hour."[2]

In April 1866, the Fourteenth Amendment was proposed to give African Americans full citizenship. Suffragists campaigned for the wording to be changed to include women as well. However, others feared that adding women to an already controversial amendment would make it more difficult to pass. They even specifically inserted the phrase about the rights of "male inhabitants."[3] It was a gender-specific designation that was not found in other parts of the United States Constitution. Stanton responded: "If the word 'male' be inserted in the Constitution, it will take us a century at least to get it out."[4] She felt excluding black women from the Fourteenth Amendment was a new form of slavery. However, Congress passed the amendment in June 1866. It would be ratified two years later.

PARTNERSHIPS AND SPLITS

In 1866, at the height of the controversy over the Fourteenth Amendment, women's rights supporters held a new convention. At the convention, a new organization called the American Equal Rights Association was formed. This group hoped to combine the Anti-Slavery Society with women's rights issues. However, most members of the group supported the passage of the Fourteenth Amendment. On the other side, were leaders such as Stanton and Anthony who did not support an amendment that excluded women.

Suffrage had begun to lose some of its long-term supporters, partly

Travels in Kansas

Stone and Blackwell traveled throughout Kansas to raise support for the referendum that could give the vote to women. Blackwell wrote to Stanton and Anthony about their travels, "You will be glad to know that Lucy and I are going over the length and breadth of this State speaking every day, and sometimes twice, journeying from twenty-five to forty miles daily, sometimes in a carriage and sometimes in an open wagon, with or without springs. We climb hills and dash down ravines, ford creeks, and ferry over rivers, rattle across limestone ledges, struggle through muddy bottoms, fight the high winds on the high rolling upland prairies, and address the most astonishing (and astonished) audiences in the most extraordinary places. . . . Kansas is to be the battle ground for 1867. It must not be allowed to fail."[5]

because of the methods used to seek a change in the amendment. Newspaper editor Horace Greeley, who had supported suffrage in his newspaper for many years, withdrew his support. Then, the cause suffered another political blow. The state of Kansas held a referendum vote in 1867 asking voters to consider two proposals: give the vote to African Americans and give the vote to women. Despite lobbying by many members of the suffrage movement who traveled to Kansas, both measures were defeated. Things were looking bleak for the suffrage movement.

In 1868, a new amendment to the Constitution was brought before Congress. The Fifteenth Amendment specifically states that the "right of citizens of the United States to vote shall not be denied or abridged by the United States or by any state on account of race, color, or previous condition of servitude."[6] The wording of the amendment reignited the controversy as suffragists argued for the insertion of the word sex along with race and color. But once again, political figures focused on giving African Americans the vote, not women. This would spark a major change in the suffrage movement.

GOING THEIR SEPARATE WAYS

The question of the Fifteenth Amendment resulted in a split among suffrage supporters. Those who were more radical, such as Stanton and Anthony, strongly and publicly opposed the amendment. Those who were less radical, such as Stone and Blackwell, supported the amendment. They felt they should honor ties to the abolition movement. Other issues divided the groups as well, such as Stanton's opinions on marriage and divorce. Stanton's association with the controversial railroad financier George Francis Train, who supported women's suffrage but disapproved of giving African Americans the vote, also created controversy. Stanton herself started to make negative comments about blacks, Asians, and other immigrants to the United States. She argued that suffrage should be for those who

Lyceums

Before the invention of radio and television, one of the most popular forms of entertainment, particularly in small towns, was the lyceum. It consisted of a series of public lectures, and it was an excellent way to spread the word about suffrage and other controversial topics. Both Anthony and Stanton took part in lyceum tours, which gave the suffrage issue needed publicity and raised money for the cause from the speakers' fees the women received. Stanton said, "I have made $2,000 since the idle of November [1870] . . . besides stirring up women generally to rebellion."[7]

were educated and familiar with US customs and traditions.

George Francis Train

George Francis Train, who worked with Stanton and Anthony on the suffrage cause, was a divisive figure because of his opinions toward African Americans. He was wealthy, having made money in railroads. The speeches he gave were often racist, and he was firmly against allowing African Americans to vote. He did support suffrage, and Anthony appeared with him at rallies in Kansas during the referendum about allowing women to vote. He divided the suffrage supporters because people such as William Lloyd Garrison and Lucy Stone hated him. Garrison said that he was "mortified and astonished beyond measure in seeing Elizabeth Cady Stanton and Susan B. Anthony traveling about the country with that crack-brained harlequin."[8]

However, Train provided funds Stanton and Anthony desperately needed, especially to help them start their own newspaper, the *Revolution*, which appeared in January 1868. Anthony admitted that Train was not always a pleasant man, but she felt it was worthwhile to deal with him because he was willing to fund and support the cause. Train's involvement in suffrage would be short-lived, however, as he soon left the country and shifted his attention to issues in Ireland. He ended up in a British prison and the *Revolution* struggled on without him for two years before going bankrupt.

Ultimately, the suffrage movement split into two separate organizations. In 1869, Stanton and Anthony formed the National Woman's Suffrage Association (NWSA). It was dedicated to suffrage above all and opposed the Fifteenth Amendment as written. That same year, Stone organized her own group, the American Woman Suffrage Association

(AWSA). According to Stone, the AWSA would "unite those who cannot use the methods, and means, which Mrs. Stanton and Susan use."[9]

A FAILED AMENDMENT

The split into the NWSA and the AWSA destroyed the unity of the suffrage movement at a time when the hope for women's suffrage was already reduced. With Stanton's support, Anthony drafted an amendment that would specifically give women the right to vote. US Congressman George Julian, a radical Republican, introduced the bill to Congress as a draft in 1869. Julian believed that all citizens should enjoy the right to vote without any distinction as to gender. The moderate suffragists opposed the amendment simply because they felt it would slow the passage of the Fifteenth Amendment. They urged a delay in proposing a specific amendment for women's suffrage.

The amendment, which would later be known as the Susan B. Anthony Amendment, stalled in Congress and was never approved. Meanwhile, the Fifteenth Amendment passed without any alteration to its language to include women, giving African Americans the right to vote. It seemed that the goal of suffrage for women was further away than ever before. ⌒

Stone formed the AWSA, a less radical group than the NWSA.

*Women were allowed to vote in a local
Wyoming Territory election in 1869.*

COMING TOGETHER

he division in the suffrage movement
resulted in two organizations—the AWSA
and the NWSA—by 1869. It seemed the issue
was going to be lost in the two groups' opposing
viewpoints. The AWSA welcomed male members.

It focused more on state referenda allowing women to vote rather than a national constitutional amendment. The AWSA also founded a publication called the *Woman's Journal*, which outlasted the NWSA's newspaper the *Revolution*. Above all, the AWSA was a more conservative group. Members were determined to ignore side issues such as divorce, religion, and birth control, and focus on suffrage.

The NWSA, under the leadership of Anthony and Stanton, continued to be a more radical organization. They were determined to keep control of the group in women's hands. The NWSA kept its focus on a national amendment for suffrage, although members did spend time on state elections. This group was more likely to be involved in controversial issues such as women's rights in marriage and divorce.

SMALL STEPS IN THE WEST

Despite the differences between the two major suffrage groups, suffrage itself was starting to make

Stanton and Anthony

Despite their long friendship working together for the suffrage cause, by the late 1860s, Stanton's involvement in the movement had become sporadic. She often took long breaks from the suffrage cause, leaving Anthony to run the NWSA on her own. Anthony complained about Stanton, telling her, "There was never such a suicidal letting go the helm of a ship in a stormy sea as had been yours these last two years."[1] By the 1880s, Stanton had stopped going on lecture tours, spending more time with her children in Europe, whereas Anthony continued to tour for suffrage well into her seventies.

One of the more unusual personalities of the suffrage movement was Victoria Woodhull. She married, divorced, remarried, had relationships outside of marriage, and had two children, only one of whom she kept. She had been arrested for prostitution and fraud but eventually befriended the wealthy Cornelius Vanderbilt and made money in stocks and real estate. Woodhull announced her candidacy for president of the United States in 1870—long before any woman had the right to vote—and many suffrage leaders admired the way her actions brought suffrage issues into the spotlight. Unfortunately, Woodhull set back the reputation of the suffrage movement when she exposed an affair by two suffrage group members.

some small gains in the western frontier. In 1869, the Wyoming Territory was the first part of the country to grant women the right to vote. Of course, since Wyoming was not a state, this historic decision did not receive a great deal of attention. Nonetheless, it set a precedent.

Over the next few decades, many other western territories and states would grant women the right to vote. Historians think men in the West were more likely to see women as equals because women were so important and such equal partners in settling the frontier. People who emigrated to the West also tended to be more liberal and less likely to follow established ways of thinking. They also disliked the interference of outsiders. Since the national suffrage organizations paid little attention to states, this probably worked in favor of suffrage.

TESTING, TESTING . . .

Not only were suffragists working to create new laws favorable to women voters, they also made their efforts more direct. Many women decided to test the voting laws in their areas. They hoped to be arrested for illegal voting so they could pursue their legal case all the way to the US Supreme Court. These suffragists hoped to prove in court that the Fourteenth and Fifteenth Amendments also gave women the right to vote.

During the presidential election of 1872, Anthony managed to register a group of women to vote. They expected

Suffragists in Court

Anthony hoped that by testing voting rights and getting arrested for illegal voting, she would get the opportunity to appear before the Supreme Court and women might win suffrage that way. While this did not happen, a suffragist did get that far in 1872.

Virginia Minor, who was president and founder of the Missouri Women Suffrage Association in 1876, brought a lawsuit against election inspectors in her state after she was prevented from voting. The Supreme Court ruled against her, claiming the US Constitution did not grant anyone the right to vote. States were responsible for regulating voting. All the Supreme Court could do was prevent certain types of discrimination. Since the Fourteenth and Fifteenth Amendments prohibit voting discrimination on the basis of race only and do not specify gender, women did not have the right to vote. The ruling was a disappointment to suffragists, but it showed them the only way to change voting laws was through the individual states or by a national amendment. They could no longer hope for a Supreme Court legal decision that would result in giving women the right to vote.

The NWSA held a convention in Chicago in 1880.
Ten years later, the NWSA and AWSA merged.

to be denied the right to vote on Election Day.
Surprisingly, they were allowed to vote. However,
they were arrested several weeks later for illegal
voting. Anthony was put in jail until a judge she
had consulted before voting, Henry R. Selden, paid
her bail and arranged for her release. Awaiting her
trial, Anthony gave speeches about her arrest and the
injustices the government committed against women.
Anthony's case did not make it to the Supreme
Court. Instead, she was deemed guilty at her trial
and given a monetary fine, which she refused to pay.

In the West, suffrage continued on an uneven course. Some states and territories such as Utah and Washington in 1870 granted women the right to vote. However, they later rescinded that decision. But some progress was made, especially in allowing women limited voting rights. By 1890, 19 states had enacted some sort of partial suffrage, usually allowing women to vote on issues such as education or alcohol reform. While these were positive steps, many suffrage leaders felt it was an easy way for states and politicians to pretend to support suffrage without actually granting women full rights.

RECONCILIATION

In 1890, reconciliation took place among suffrage supporters. The NWSA and the AWSA merged and suffrage was reunited under one organization. The philosophies that had divided the groups were no longer as different. The new organization, known as the National American Woman Suffrage Association (NAWSA), tried to stay clear of more controversial subjects and focus on suffrage alone.

Meanwhile, other popular causes for women gained strength and affected how some people viewed suffrage. Suffrage had always been linked with the temperance movement. Many suffrage supporters were also temperance supporters. The National Women's Christian Temperance Union (WCTU) was the most powerful women's group in the country. Its leader, Frances Willard, supported women's suffrage and brought many other women with her to the cause. Temperance was a tricky subject, however. Many businessmen involved in industries connected to alcohol, such as distilleries and saloons, believed giving women the vote would allow them to pass antialcohol legislation.

While suffrage supporters were enjoying reconciliation, other organizations were forming to oppose suffrage. In the mid-1890s, these groups grew, claiming that a woman's place was in the home and voting would erode the traditional structure of the family. They also claimed that women's votes would not be worth much. Many pointed out that women

Abigail Scott Duniway

One of the most prominent suffragists in the West was Abigail Scott Duniway. She had traveled west on the Oregon Trail at the age of 17. Duniway founded the Oregon State Equal Suffrage Association in 1873. She frequently traveled to campaign for suffrage, and in 1883, she was a witness when the Washington territorial legislature gave women the right to vote. Doris Weatherford describes the scene in her book *A History of the American Suffragist Movement*: She went up from Oregon on the big day and with "trembling hands" recorded each legislator's vote. When the victory was clear, she rushed to the telegraph office, "my feet seeming to tread the air. A bloodless battle had been fought and won."[2]

who already had the right to vote had not exercised it in elections. Although many suffrage supporters felt these antisuffrage groups were just a cover for the liquor industry, the movement grew. In 1911, the antisuffrage people formed the National Association Opposed to Woman Suffrage. By 1916, it would boast 350,000 members.

The End of an Era

As the 1800s drew to a close, the first suffrage leaders were slowly fading away. Stone died in 1893. Stanton died in 1902, and Anthony died in 1906. With their deaths, the first phase of the suffrage movement came to an end. The NAWSA was suffering from low membership and a lack of funds. The organization's new president, Carrie Chapman Catt, was not optimistic about the NAWSA's chances for success. She blamed the members, saying the greatest challenge to the movement was "the hopeless, lifeless, faithless members of our own organization. 'It cannot be done' is their favorite motto."[3] Clearly, the movement's leaders needed to breathe new life into the suffrage issue. Catt, and her successor, Anna Howard Shaw, reached out to affluent women to support the cause of suffrage.

These women had the time and energy—and money—
to devote to the suffrage movement.

The NAWSA also supported the new Women's
Trade Union League in 1903 to make a connection
with working-class women. The Industrial
Revolution had brought a demand for factory
laborers, so more women left their homes to work in
locations such as textile mills and clothing factories.
Women were now working outside the home for
wages. Many young women were leaving home and
living on their own. Because of their
increasing independence, as well
as terrible work conditions some
encountered, some women became
more eager to have a political voice
through voting.

With the rise of the Industrial
Revolution, suffrage was entering
a new era, with new leadership and
new tactics. Women were more
determined than ever to make their
voices heard to gain the right to vote.
It would take more creative methods
than those of the suffrage pioneers to
accomplish this. —

Woman's Journal

The *Woman's Journal* publication of the AWSA, which started in January 1870, would be one of the most lasting voices for suffrage. It would also benefit from contributions from noteworthy writers, including Harriet Beecher Stowe, who wrote the famous antislavery novel *Uncle Tom's Cabin*, and Louisa May Alcott, best known for *Little Women*. The *Woman's Journal* was published until 1917, when it was replaced by the *Woman Citizen*.

Catt was frustrated with the lack of participation in the suffrage movement when she was president of the NAWSA.

Chapter 7

Many female workers became interested in suffrage.

By Whatever Means Necessary

As the nineteenth century became the twentieth century, suffrage entered a new era. The suffrage movement was 50 years old. Many of the women who had pioneered the fight were gone. A new generation of suffragists was taking up the cause. These new suffragists were using more dramatic methods to publicize their cause and make their voices heard.

REACHING OUT

Suffragists continued to reach out to working women in the early 1900s. Social reformer Jane Addams, who had founded settlement houses in Chicago to help new immigrants and working women with services such as child care and classes, was a strong supporter of suffrage. She felt the ability to vote could only improve the lives of working-class women. Another suffrage supporter who believed in reaching out to working women was Harriot Stanton Blatch, the daughter of Elizabeth Cady Stanton. Blatch had been living in England, where she participated in the British movement for women's suffrage. There, the movement had made an effort to include working

The Triangle Tragedy

An event that pointed out the need for women to vote as a way to have a voice in laws that directly concerned their safety was the Triangle Shirtwaist Factory fire on March 25, 1911. Triangle was a garment factory that employed many young women, most of them Eastern-European Jewish immigrants. When the fire broke out, the women were unable to escape because the exit doors were locked—it was a way for the owners to prevent theft. The women perished in the flames or leaped from windows. More than 140 died. As a result of the fire, many working women realized they would only have a say in improving working conditions if they were able to vote.

women. When Blatch returned to
the United States, she formed the
Equality League of Self-Supporting
Women to promote voting rights for
working women.

But as the new century moved
forward, suffragists realized the polite
and conservative methods they had
used in the past—such as conventions,
petitions, and newspapers—were no
longer going to work. It was time for
more radical methods that would get
suffragists the attention they needed.
They had won some small victories as
women gained the vote in 15 states by
the end of the 1910s. It was time to
press the issue.

A Radical Leader

Just in time for the newer radical
methods, a woman returned to the
United States from England ready
to take up the cause of suffrage for
US women. Her name was Alice
Paul. Paul would become one of

Emmeline Pankhurst

One of Alice Paul's
inspirations for the US
suffrage movement was
Emmeline Pankhurst, who
led the British suffrage
movement. Her tactics
included staging disrup-
tive protests that would
allow the suffragettes,
as they were known in
England, to be arrested.
Then, they would con-
duct hunger strikes. Paul
joined Pankhurst's group,
the Women's Social and
Political Union, when she
was attending graduate
school in England in 1909
and was jailed several
times. Paul learned most
of her tactics of militant
protest from Pankhurst
and her group.

Alice Paul, 1918

the most important people in bringing about the
passage of an amendment for women's suffrage. As a
graduate student in England, Paul had participated
in demonstrations, been arrested and jailed, and
went on hunger strikes. When she returned to the
United States in 1910, she joined the NAWSA. She

Women march in a parade in Washington DC on March 3, 1913.

proposed a new suffrage strategy: to openly oppose
the president and his political party until he agreed
that women should have the vote. Paul explained her
stance on suffrage:

> *To me there is nothing complicated about ordinary equality.*
> *We women of America tell you that America is not a*
> *democracy. Twenty million women are denied the right to*
> *vote.*[1]

One method employed for calling attention
to the cause was to stage large-scale marches. The

largest march yet took place in Washington DC on March 3, 1913. Eight thousand women participated in this march, following the same route as the president's inaugural parade. Led by attorney Inez Milholland, dressed in all white and riding a white horse, the women were divided into groups based on their occupations. There were six groups: farmers, homemakers, actresses, librarians, doctors, and college students. Each woman wore a uniform or costume illustrating her group. A huge banner proclaimed, "We demand an amendment to the Constitution of the United States enfranchising the women of the country."[2]

Another Split

However, differences of opinion concerning the tactics used for the suffrage movement caused another split. Paul's followers formed the

Inez Milholland

Milholland led the suffrage parade in Washington DC, and she would later become the martyr of the movement. In 1916, she went on a tour of the western states, promoting suffrage, even though she was ill with tonsillitis and anemia. In October, Milholland collapsed while speaking to a crowd in Los Angeles. According to legend, she had just said, "How long must women wait for liberty?"[3] She died a month later.

Congressional Union (CU), which used more radical tactics. The NAWSA continued to be more conservative in its approach to gaining suffrage, focusing on political strategy. This time, however, the two wings of the suffrage movement worked well together. The CU, which eventually became the National Woman's Party, used more radical tactics, while the NAWSA focused on political methods.

World War I (1914–1918) was also looming over the United States. As they were during the Civil War, suffragists were forced to decide whether their efforts should be shelved during the war. Or should the fight for women's votes continue? The United States entered the war on April 6, 1917, and the suffrage movement decided to continue its campaign. "This is a time for speeding up, not resting," NAWSA leader Catt declared.[4] However, the women also vowed to support the war by volunteering in the Red Cross and selling War Savings Stamps. They hoped their support would show they were loyal Americans and worthy of the right to vote.

The Susan B. Anthony Amendment

Although the Susan B. Anthony Amendment had not passed in 1869 as the sixteenth amendment, it continued to be brought before the US Congress. However, each time, it fell short of the two-thirds majority needed for passage. In late September 1917, the US House of Representatives agreed to create the Committee on Woman Suffrage. This was an important step in bringing the Susan B. Anthony Amendment for a vote again. In November 1917, the Rules Committee of the House of Representatives announced that the amendment would again come before Congress on January 10, 1918, this time as the Nineteenth

Sara Bard Field

One of the memorable tactics used to promote suffrage was the coast-to-coast journey of Sara Bard Field in 1915. The Panama-Pacific International Exposition had just taken place in San Francisco, California, and suffragists had collected 500,000 signatures on a women's rights petition. Paul decided it would be a great publicity stunt if the petition was delivered to the president in Washington via a cross-country car trip. Field, a poet and suffrage supporter, was chosen by Paul to make the trip along with two Swedish women who had purchased a new car in California and were returning to Rhode Island. They left in September 1915. At this time, driving was still in its infancy and the trip was difficult. Breakdowns were frequent, and the car often became stuck in muddy roads. Field's two companions were also difficult for her to get along with. But along the way, Field gave speeches in small towns and collected more signatures, including those of prominent politicians and governors. The trip also increased public knowledge of the suffrage cause to people who otherwise were unaware of it and created more supporters. Field finally reached Washington in December and gave the petition to President Woodrow Wilson.

A Hunger Striker

Paul was not the only suffragist who went on a hunger strike while jailed. One of the women who was jailed for suffrage protests and endured force-feeding was Rose Winslow. Winslow managed to write down her observations on small pieces of paper that were smuggled out of the prison. She wrote about being force-fed: "I had a nervous time of it, gasping a long time afterward and my stomach rejecting during the process. I spent a bad, restless night, but otherwise I am all right. The poor soul who fed me got liberally besprinkled during the process. I heard myself making the most hideous sounds. . . . One feels so forsaken when one lies prone and people shove a pipe down one's stomach."[6]

Amendment to the Constitution. Opposition was still fierce and the vote was uncertain, so the suffragists continued their efforts.

PROTESTING

The CU, now called the National Women's Party (NWP), continued its efforts during the war. Paul was determined that all of the group's work would continue, including a series of controversial protests in front of the White House. Throughout the winter of 1917, Paul and her supporters staged silent protests in front of the White House. The women stood at the gates with signs that read, "Mr. President, How Long Must Women Wait for Liberty?"[5] The suffragists were silent, protesting only with signs and their presence. Over time, their signs became more critical of President Woodrow Wilson, especially as the United States became involved in World War I. The suffragists felt President Wilson was a hypocrite for sending

US men to die overseas to protect democracy while women at home were denied voting rights and that same democracy. However, this tended to turn public opinion against them. Some people considered the women unpatriotic.

SENT TO JAIL

Soon, the protestors were being attacked by spectators and then arrested on charges of obstructing traffic. At first, the charges were dropped. But as the protests continued, women were being sent to jail. Eventually, Paul was arrested, tried, and sentenced to seven months in jail. Conditions were terrible in the prison for Paul. She was kept in solitary confinement with only bread and water to eat. Weakened and unable to walk, she was sent to the prison infirmary. There, she started a hunger strike. "It was the strongest weapon left with which to continue . . . our battle," she later said.[7] Doctors finally placed her in a psychiatric ward. They force-fed her by pouring liquids into her stomach through a tube stuck down her throat. Despite the pain, Paul refused to end her hunger strike.

After five weeks in prison, Paul was set free. But Paul was just one of the jailed women participating in the hunger strike. Others had also been arrested and were following Paul's techniques. Newspaper stories about the conditions in the jail and the force-feeding of the suffrage protestors created more support for the suffrage movement. The NAWSA, meanwhile, had convinced the president and other politicians that suffrage was important to the war effort. It seemed that suffrage was finally within grasp. But the battle had not yet been won. ⌐

Female college students protest in front of the White House in February 1917.

President Wilson put his support behind women's suffrage in 1918.

THE DAWN OF A NEW ERA

he Nineteenth Amendment, which would
guarantee women the right to vote, was
to be voted on in Congress on January 10, 1918.
Suffragists hoped President Wilson had enough
political power to push the amendment through

Congress to approval. The first test would be in the US House of Representatives, and it did not look good. The opposition succeeded in slowing the progress of the bill and moving the vote to October.

Finally, on October 1, 1918, the Nineteenth Amendment was brought before Congress. Just before the vote, President Wilson said, "I regard the extension of suffrage to women as vitally essential to the successful prosecution of the great war of humanity in which we are engaged."[1] But even with the president's vocal support of suffrage, the amendment was two votes short of passing.

Suffragists tried not to be discouraged. They realized that with a congressional election about to take place, just a few new pro-suffrage senators could make the difference in passing the amendment the next time it came up for a vote. The NAWSA began a campaign against two senators

Charlotte Woodward Pierce

When the Nineteenth Amendment was ratified, only one woman who had attended the first women's rights convention in Seneca Falls, New York, was still alive. Charlotte Woodward Pierce was only 19 when she attended that first convention, and she was 91 when women won the right to vote. When the NWP was building its headquarters in Washington DC in 1921, Pierce sent a trowel to be used in laying the cornerstone. It was inscribed, "In memory of the Seneca Falls Convention in 1848: presented by its sole survivor, Mrs. Charlotte L. Pierce, in thanksgiving for progress made by women and in honor of the National Woman's Party, which will carry on the struggle so bravely begun."[2]

League of Women Voters

Once suffrage was achieved, the NAWSA transformed into the League of Women Voters, an organization whose goals would include fostering good government, doing public service, and supporting feminist issues. Ninety years later, the league is still active in promoting citizen involvement in government. In 2010, the group's mission statement read, "The League of Women Voters, a nonpartisan political organization, encourages informed and active participation in government, works to increase understanding of major public policy issues, and influences public policy through education and advocacy."[3]

who were against suffrage, helping to prevent their election. This sent the message that the suffrage issue was one that could make or break an election for a candidate. This may have helped persuade other senators to think carefully about their stand on the issue.

The Nineteenth Amendment was proposed before Congress again in January 1919. The vote was scheduled for that summer. President Wilson again applied his political pressure to gain support for the bill. In June, the Nineteenth Amendment was approved by the House and then the Senate. Ratification by three-fourths of the states—a total of 36 states— was needed for the amendment to become part of the Constitution.

IN THE HANDS OF THE STATES

Now came the most difficult time for suffrage supporters. The NAWSA and the NWP joined to form

*Paul made a huge banner on which she sewed a star for every state
that ratified the Nineteenth Amendment.*

ratification committees all over the country. They
hoped to use lobbying and publicity to bring about
passage of the amendment in their respective states.
It took only a week for the first two states, Michigan
and Wisconsin, to ratify the amendment. By March
1920, 35 states had ratified the amendment. Only
one state remained to reach the goal.

It was not easy to find that last state. Most of the states that had not ratified the amendment were conservative and less likely to approve of suffrage. The suffrage movement settled on Tennessee as the state where suffragists would concentrate their ratification efforts. Both suffrage and antisuffrage groups converged on the state, each trying to sway the state's politicians to its side.

THE FINAL BATTLE

On August 9, 1920, Tennessee's Governor Albert Roberts called the legislative session to order, saying, "Millions of women are looking

---

One Last Conference

In March 1919, the NAWSA held conventions in large cities throughout the United States, marking 50 years since the organization was formed. There had been many conventions since 1869, but with suffrage in sight, the whole character of the conventions had changed since those early days. According to attendee Ida Husted Harper,

> There were no longer eloquent pleas and arguments for the ballot. . . . Now there was business and political consideration of the best and quickest methods of bringing the movement to an end and the most effective use that could be made of the suffrage already so largely won. It was a little difficult for some of the older workers to accustom themselves to the change, which deprived the convention of its old-time crusading, consecrated spirit, but the younger ones were full of ardor and enthusiasm over the limitless opportunities that were within their grasp.[4]

In the closing speech at one convention, Anna Howard Shaw said, "The suffragist who has not been mobbed has nothing really interesting to look back upon."[5]

to this Legislature to give them a voice and share in shaping the destiny of the Republic."[6] At first, things seemed to go smoothly as the Tennessee Senate voted overwhelmingly in favor of the amendment. But the House Speaker, Seth M. Walker, brought things to a halt when he adjourned the session after seeing that his antisuffrage side was going to lose. By adjourning, he was giving the antisuffragists more time to sway the pro-suffrage politicians.

Catt later said of the events in Nashville,

Never in the history of politics has there been . . . such a nefarious lobby as labored to block the ratification in Nashville, Tenn. In the short time I spent in Tennessee's capital, I have been called more names, been more maligned, more lied about than in the thirty previous years I worked for suffrage. I was flooded with anonymous letters, vulgar, ignorant, insane.[7]

August 18 dawned hot and tense. Some suffragist supporters went to extraordinary lengths to cast their votes. One come from his hospital bed and another stepped off a train that was about to leave the station and take him to his dying child. The vote was 48–48. This tie would mean defeat for the amendment.

One Vote

Suddenly, a young legislator named Harry Burn, only 24 years old, remembered that he had promised his mother that if there were a tie, he would vote for suffrage. His vote passed the amendment. When an antisuffrage group claimed Burn had been bribed, he asked that the following statement be officially recorded in the legislative proceedings:

> *I changed my vote in favor of ratification because I believe in full suffrage as a right; . . . I know that a mother's advice is always safest for her boy to follow and my mother wanted me to vote for ratification.*[8]

With Burn's vote, US women had won the right to vote. Despite a few more last-gasp efforts by antisuffragists, Governor Roberts mailed the official certificate of ratification to Washington DC on

Female Representative

The election of 1916 was a landmark for suffrage supporters when Jeannette Rankin was elected to the US House of Representatives by the state of Montana. She was a former employee of the NAWSA, but her campaign emphasized peace, so she was supported by both the NAWSA and the NWP. Suffragists delighted in pointing out that before US women could even vote, Montanans had so much faith in the abilities of women that they elected one to the nation's highest lawmaking group.

Harry Burn

August 24. When it was received on August 26, Secretary of State Bainbridge Colby declared that the Nineteenth Amendment to the US Constitution

had been ratified. Women's suffrage was finally
a reality.

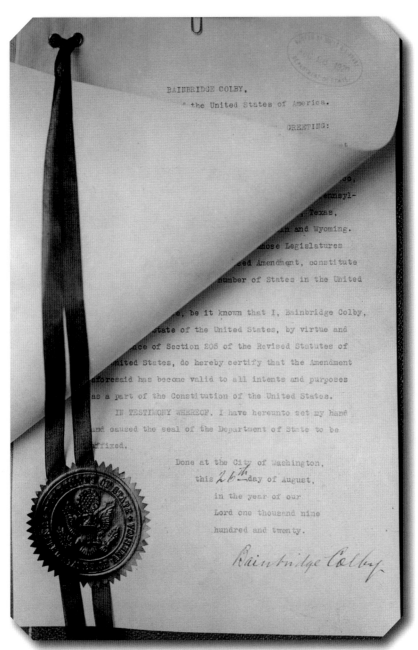

BAINBRIDGE COLBY,

the United States of America.

GREETING:

Pennsyl-

Texas,

and Wyoming.

hose Legislatures

sed Amendment, constitute

number of States in the United

be it known that I, Bainbridge Colby,

State of the United States, by virtue and

ce of Section 205 of the Revised Statutes of

United States, do hereby certify that the Amendment

aforesaid has become valid to all intents and purposes

as a part of the Constitution of the United States.

IN TESTIMONY WHEREOF. I have hereunto set my hand

and caused the seal of the Department of State to be

affixed.

Done at the City of Washington,

this 26th day of August,

in the year of our

Lord one thousand nine

hundred and twenty.

Bainbridge Colby

A facsimile of the certificate of ratification
which was signed by Bainbridge Colby

People march in Washington DC during the women's liberation movement of the 1970s.

THE LEGACY OF SUFFRAGE

It has been nearly a century since the women's suffrage movement achieved its goal and the Nineteenth Amendment was ratified. Since then, women have made great progress in what they can do and what their place is in society, but there are still areas where they struggle for acceptance and equality. In fact, the suffrage movement led to more campaigns for women's rights.

However, many historians argue that allowing women to vote made no real difference in the political makeup of the United States. Some feel women's voices became weaker once they joined the existing political parties, while others feel it was natural for women's influence to be less distinctive once they became part of the overall voting population. The League of Women Voters, which evolved out of the NAWSA, even shifted its focus from shaping political policy to emphasizing voter education and helping women become responsible voters.

The Equal Rights Amendment

In the 1960s and 1970s, women began to seek new forms of equality. This spawned a feminist movement called the women's liberation movement, or women's lib. Society had shifted away from women occupying the home and raising children, and women were looking for more choices and more equality in the workplace. The new feminist movement resulted in the proposal of a new amendment to the Constitution known as the Equal Rights Amendment (ERA). It stated simply that "equality of rights under the law shall not be denied or abridged by the United States or by any State on account of sex."[1] The ERA actually passed in Congress in 1972, but it was never able to gain enough support from the states and expired in June 1982 three states short of ratification. The conservative element of the United States was growing. Many people thought the ERA would force too many changes in the roles of men and women. However, the ERA was not a total loss. As author Jane Mansbridge stated,

> *The ERA campaign produced support— and angry support, the kind that brings with it money and volunteer time—among women and men who had never belonged to a feminist, or even a reformist, organization. Having been touched by*

Alice Paul

In the 1970s, when feminists were struggling to get the ERA ratified, Paul was still very much involved, though she was in her eighties. Paul had never wavered from her goal of achieving equality for women, and even as feminism evolved, she feared that women would never achieve full equality without getting rid of laws that discriminated against them. She rewrote the ERA into the form sent for ratification to reflect elements of the Nineteenth Amendment. She died in 1977, still fighting for the ERA and women's rights.

the ERA, these citizens began to pay more attention to other issues on the feminist agenda. The ratification struggle probably increased the energy and resources available for other feminist causes rather than harming those causes.[2]

Although the ERA was not ratified, the roles of women in society have continually widened since the 1980s, which is especially impressive since this had also been a time of conservative politics and fewer radical reform movements. There have been many firsts for women since that time, including the first woman in space (astronaut Sally Ride), a female secretary of state (Condoleezza Rice), women participating in combat positions in the military, and women running for high office, such as vice president and president of the United States. Women now sit on the Supreme Court, are state governors, and run corporations.

Gloria Steinem

Gloria Steinem became widely known in the 1960s and 1970s as the leader of the women's liberation movement. She has written many books on feminist issues. She founded *Ms.* magazine, was a spokesperson for the movement, and has been a supporter of abortion rights. She also cofounded the Women's Media Center in 2005 to strengthen the voices of women in media. Steinem is called a radical feminist and her views are frequently controversial, but she remains a symbol of the feminist movement who helped bring about changes in the roles of US women.

More Work To Be Done

Women have not achieved all of their goals,
however. There is still a glass ceiling in the workplace
that prevents many women from achieving the
highest positions. Women also tend to be paid less
than men for the
same jobs, in some
cases making only
three-quarters as
much as men do
for the same work.
Women may also be
denied promotions
and raises if they
take time off to
have children.
Gender roles are
still an issue. Many
women struggle
against the societal
expectation that
they have full-time
careers to support
themselves and still
bear the largest

A Woman for President

In addition to getting the right to vote, many
suffragists hoped to have more of a voice in
US politics. In fact, two women ran campaigns
for president during the suffrage era. In 1872,
Victoria Woodhull announced she was running for president. Even her fellow suffragists
were surprised, but Woodhull did not have any
expectations of winning. She simply saw it as a
way to raise issues related to suffrage and gain
attention for the cause.

In 1880 and 1884, attorney Belva Lockwood
also ran for president from the National Equal
Rights Party. Like Woodhull, she did not expect
to win but saw the campaign as a way to get
attention for the cause. She also hoped to
elect a woman to one seat in the Electoral College—which chooses the president—as a way
to get women into the political process. She
had some support from voters in the West who
were more open to women's suffrage. Though
she failed, Lockwood felt it was an important
step to take, saying, "We shall never have
equal rights until we take them, nor respect
until we command it."[3]

burden when it comes to housework and child care. Reproductive rights also continue to be an issue, such as a woman's right to have an abortion. In religion, women are still barred from holding high positions in many churches. The Roman Catholic Church does not allow women to become priests. Women in politics still fall behind the male majority, although their numbers have increased. And, as of 2011, the United States had never elected a female president.

Women are still struggling to be perceived and treated as equals to men in US society, but the suffrage movement serves as an example of what can be achieved. Almost 100 years after finally getting the right to vote, it may be easy for women to take that right for granted, but suffrage is just one step along a path to women's roles in the twenty-first century. As Stanton once said,

Lucy Burns

Not every woman who devoted large portions of her life to achieving suffrage was happy about it afterward. Some were tired and bitter, especially when the expected changes in society did not take place just because women could vote. One suffragist Lucy Burns was particularly disheartened about women who never participated in the suffrage movement at all. "I don't want to do anything more," she said. "I think we have done all this for women, and we have sacrificed everything we possessed for them, and now let them . . . fight for it. I am not going to fight anymore."[4]

"[Throughout history] there are so many brave and headstrong women who refused to do the prudent things and died failures in their own time. Now we put their pictures on stamps and name roads and schools in their honor. We stand on their shoulders and tell our children their stories."[6]

—*Gail Collins,*
America's Women

Our successors . . . have big work before them—much bigger, in fact, than they imagine. We are only the stone that started the ripple, but they are the ripple that is spreading and will eventually cover the whole pond.[5] ⌐

Hillary Clinton was a presidential hopeful in the 2008 elections. As of 2011, the United States had never had a female president.

Timeline

1840	1848	1850
In June, Lucretia Mott and Elizabeth Cady Stanton are barred from participation in the World Anti-Slavery Convention.	The Seneca Falls Convention takes place in Seneca Falls, New York, on July 19 and 20.	A women's rights convention is held in Salem, Ohio, on April 19 and 20.

1866	1866	1867
The American Equal Rights Association is formed on May 10.	In June, Congress approves the Fourteenth Amendment, calling for strengthening African-American voting rights.	In November, a referendum is held in Kansas for women's suffrage. The issue fails.

1850	1851	1852
The First National Women's Rights Convention is held in Worcester, Massachusetts, on October 23 and 24.	Sojourner Truth speaks at a women's rights convention in Akron, Ohio.	Susan B. Anthony joins the suffrage movement.

1868	1869	1869
The Fourteenth Amendment is ratified on July 28.	On January 19, Anthony proposes a sixteenth amendment to give women the right to vote.	Suffrage supporters split into two organizations: the NWSA and the AWSA.

TIMELINE

1869	1870	1870
The Wyoming Territory grants women the right to vote on December 10.	The Utah Territory approves women's suffrage on February 10.	The Fifteenth Amendment becomes part of the Constitution on March 30.

1910	1913	1917
Alice Paul joins the NAWSA.	On March 3, 1913, 8,000 women march in a suffrage parade in Washington DC.	Female protestors begin picketing the White House on January 10.

1872

On November 5, women across the country test voting laws by attempting to vote. Many are later arrested.

1875

On March 20, the Supreme Court rules that the Fourteenth and Fifteenth Amendments do not give women the right to vote.

1890

The NWSA and the AWSA merge to form the NAWSA.

1919

Congress passes the Nineteenth Amendment on June 14. The first states ratify the amendment.

1920

Tennessee becomes the thirty-sixth state to ratify the Nineteenth Amendment on August 18.

1920

On August 26, the Nineteenth Amendment officially becomes part of the Constitution, giving women the right to vote.

Essential Facts

Date of Event

Begins with the Seneca Falls Convention in Seneca Falls, New York, on April 19 and 20 in 1848. The right to vote is finally achieved with the successful ratification of the Nineteenth Amendment on August 26, 1920.

Place of Event

United States of America

Key Players

- ❖ Elizabeth Cady Stanton
- ❖ Susan B. Anthony
- ❖ Lucretia Mott
- ❖ Lucy Stone
- ❖ Alice Paul
- ❖ Carrie Chapman Catt

HIGHLIGHTS OF EVENT

❖ In 1848, the Seneca Falls Convention was held in Seneca Falls, New York. The convention drafted a list of women's rights, among the most controversial was a women's right to vote.

❖ The First National Women's Rights Convention was held in Worcester, Massachusetts, in 1850.

❖ Wyoming Territory granted women the right to vote in 1869.

❖ Congress passed the Nineteenth Amendment in 1919, giving women the right to vote.

❖ Tennessee became the thirty-sixth state to ratify the Nineteenth Amendment, officially making it a law in 1920.

QUOTE

"To me there is nothing complicated about ordinary equality. We women of America tell you that America is not a democracy. Twenty million women are denied the right to vote."—*Alice Paul*

GLOSSARY

abolition
> The process of making slavery illegal.

amendment
> An alteration or addition to the Constitution.

approbation
> Approval or commendation.

candidacy
> The process of seeking an electoral office.

controversial
> Causing a public dispute, debate, or argument.

enfranchise
> To grant someone the privileges of citizenship, especially the right to vote.

inalienable
> Something that cannot be transferred, changed, or taken away.

lyceum
> An institution that provides lectures, concerts, and discussions for the purpose of education.

parliamentary
> Following the formal methods of procedure discussion and debate in an organized assembly.

reconciliation
> The process of creating an agreement or harmony after a quarrel or dispute.

referendum
> A proposed legislative measure that is voted on by the public.

reform
> To improve or change something that is wrong, corrupt, or unsatisfactory.

resolution
> A formal expression of an opinion or intention.

successor
> A person who takes over from another in an office or position.

suffrage
> The right to vote, especially in a political election.

temperance
> Having to do with avoiding consumption of alcohol.

territory
> A region or area of the United States that has not yet become a state.

ADDITIONAL RESOURCES

SELECTED BIBLIOGRAPHY

Baker, Jean H., ed. *Votes for Women: The Struggle for Suffrage Revisited*. New York: Oxford UP, 2002. Print.

Collins, Gail. *America's Women: 400 Years of Dolls, Drudges, Helpmates, and Heroines*. New York: HarperCollins, 2003. Print.

Cott, Nancy. *The Bonds of Womanhood: "Woman's Sphere" in New England, 1780–1835*. New Haven, CT: Yale UP, 1977. Print.

Moynihan, Ruth Barnes, et al. *Second to None: A Documentary History of American Women, Volume II: From 1865 to the Present*. Lincoln, NE: U of Nebraska P, 1993. Print.

FURTHER READINGS

Bausum, Ann. *With Courage and Cloth: Winning the Fight for a Woman's Right to Vote*. Washington, DC: National Geographic, 2004. Print.

MacDonald, Fiona. *You Wouldn't Want to Be a Suffragist! A Protest Movement That's Rougher Than You Expected*. New York: Scholastic, 2008. Print.

Ruth, Janice E., and Evelyn Sinclair. *Women Who Dare: Women of the Suffrage Movement*. Washington, DC: Library of Congress, 2006. Print.

Shea, Pegi Deitz, and Iris Van Rynbach. *The Taxing Case of the Cows: A True Story About Suffrage*. New York: Clarion, 2010. Print.

Web Links

To learn more about the fight for women's suffrage, visit ABDO Publishing Company online at **www.abdopublishing.com**. Web sites about the fight for women's suffrage are featured on our Book Links page. These links are routinely monitored and updated to provide the most current information available.

Places to Visit

National Women's History Museum
205 S Whiting Street, Suite 254, Alexandria, VA 22304
703-461-1920
http://www.nwhm.org
This museum is dedicated to research, exhibits, and collections about women's history in the United States.

Sewall-Belmont House and Museum
144 Constitution Avenue NE, Washington, DC 20002-5608
202-546-1210
http://www.sewallbelmont.org
The Sewall-Belmont House is home to the headquarters and museum of the National Women's Party and includes exhibits about the suffrage movement.

Women's Rights National Historic Park
136 Fall Street, Seneca Falls, NY 13148
315-568-2991
http://www.nps.gov/wori
This park, located on the site of the first women's rights convention, includes a visitor's center and historic sites such as Elizabeth Cady Stanton's house.

SOURCE NOTES

Chapter 1. Seneca Falls
1. Jone Johnson Lewis. "Seneca Falls 1848 Women's Rights Convention." *About.com*. The New York Times Company, 2011. Web. 26 Jan. 2011.
2. Elizabeth C. Stanton, et al. *History of Woman Suffrage*. New York: Fowler & Wells, 1881. Print. 70–71.
3. Jone Johnson Lewis. "Seneca Falls 1848 Women's Rights Convention." *About.com*. The New York Times Company, 2011. Web. 26 Jan. 2011.
4. "The Seneca Falls Convention." *National Portrait Gallery*. Smithsonian Institute National Portrait Gallery, n.d. Web. 26 Jan. 2011.

Chapter 2. The Weaker Sex
1. *The Holy Bible*. Cleveland, OH: The World Publishing Company, 1962. Print. 3.
2. Gail Collins. *America's Women: 400 Years of Dolls, Drudges, Helpmates, and Heroines*. New York: Harpercollins, 2003. Print. 29.
3. Ibid. 82-83.
4. Ibid. 83.
5. Ibid.
6. Doris Weatherford. *A History of the American Suffrage Movement*. New York: MTM, 2005. Print. 9.
7. Ibid.

Chapter 3. From Abolition to Suffrage
1. Nancy F. Cott. *The Bonds of Womanhood: "Woman's Sphere" in New England, 1780-1835*. New Haven, CT: Yale UP, 1977. Print.140–141.
2. Jeff Hill. *Defining Moments: Woman's Suffrage*. Detroit: Omnigraphics, 2006. Print. 168.
3. Doris Weatherford. *A History of the American Suffrage Movement*. New York: MTM, 2005. Print.18.
4. Jeff Hill. *Defining Moments: Woman's Suffrage*. Detroit: Omnigraphics, 2006. Print. 176.
5. Ibid. 17.
6. Ibid. 175.
7. Ibid. 21.
8. Ibid. 20.

Chapter 4. Toward a Common Cause

1. Jeff Hill. *Defining Moments: Woman's Suffrage*. Detroit: Omnigraphics, 2006. Print. 22.

2. Doris Weatherford. *A History of the American Suffrage Movement*. New York: MTM, 2005. Print. 38.

3. Ibid. 42.

4. Ibid. 51.

5. Sojourner Truth. "Ain't I a Woman?" *Modern History SourceBook*. Paul Halsall, 1997. Web. 26 Jan. 2011.

6. Elizabeth Cady Stanton. *Eighty Years and More (1815-1897)*. New York: European, 1898. Print. 165.

7. Sojourner Truth. "What Time of Night It Is, 1853." *Encyclopædia Britannica*. Encyclopædia Britannica, 1881. Web. 26 Jan. 2011.

Chapter 5. Growing Pains

1. Philip S. Foner. *Frederick Douglass on Women's Rights*. New York: Da Capo, 1992. Print. 87.

2. Elizabeth C. Stanton, et al. *History of Woman Suffrage*. New York: Fowler & Wells, 1881. Print. 324.

3. Jone Johnson Lewis. "Women's History." *About.com*. The New York Times Company, 2011. Web. 3 Feb. 2011.

4. Harriet Sigerman. *Elizabeth Cady Stanton: The Right is Ours*. New York: Oxford UP, 2001. Print. 86.

5. Elizabeth Cady Stanton, Susan B. Anthony, and Matilda Joslyn Gage. *History of Woman Suffrage, Volume II*. E-book. Web.

6. "Primary Documents in American History: Fifteenth Amendment to the Constitution." *Library of Congress*. Library of Congress, 30 Jun. 2010. Web. 28 Jan. 2011.

7. Elizabeth Cady Stanton, Susan Brownell Anthony, Ann Dexter Gordon, *The Selected Papers of Elizabeth Cady Stanton and Susan B. Anthony: Against an aristocracy of sex, 1866 to 1873*. Rutgers UP, 2000. Print. 299.

8. Elizabeth C. Stanton et al., *History of Woman Suffrage*. New York: Fowler & Wells, 1881. Print. 34.

9. Ibid. 38.

Source Notes Continued

Chapter 6. Coming Together
1. Elizabeth Cady Stanton, Susan Brownell Anthony, Ann Dexter Gordon. *The Selected Papers of Elizabeth Cady Stanton and Susan B. Anthony: Against an aristocracy of sex, 1866 to 1873*. Rutgers UP, 2000. Print. 299.
2. Doris Weatherford. *A History of the American Suffrage Movement*. New York: MTM, 2005. Print. 140–141.
3. Elizabeth C. Stanton et al., *History of Woman Suffrage*. New York: Fowler & Wells, 1881. Print. 61.

Chapter 7. By Whatever Means Necessary
1. "Alice Paul Quotes," *About.com Women's History*. The New York Times Company, 2011. Web. 3 Feb. 2011.
2. Ann Bausum. *With Courage and Cloth: Winning the Fight for a Woman's Right to Vote*. Washington, DC: National Geographic Society, 2004. Print. 8.
3. "Suffrage Movement." *The Library of Congress*. The Library of Congress, 26 Sept. 2002. Web. 3 Feb. 2011.
4. Jeff Hill. *Defining Moments: Woman's Suffrage*. Detroit: Omnigraphics, 2006. Print. 78.
5. "Women and the Vote: Alice Paul's Fight for Suffrage." *PBS Kids*. WGBH Educational Foundation, 2004. Web. 3 Feb. 2011.
6. "Starving for Women's Suffrage: 'I Am Not Strong after These Weeks.'" *History Matters*. n.p., n.d. Web. 3 Feb. 2011.
7. "Women and the Vote: Alice Paul's Fight for Suffrage." *PBS Kids*. WGBH Educational Foundation, 2004. Web. 3 Feb. 2011.

Chapter 8. The Dawn of a New Era

1. "19th Amendment." *History.com.* A&E Television Networks, 2011. Web. 10 Feb. 2011.

2. "Women's Rights: Charlotte Woodward." *nps.gov.* National Park Service, 8 Sept. 2009. Web. 3 Feb. 2010.

3. "About the League: Mission Statement." *League of Women Voters.* n.p., n.d. Web. 3 Feb. 2011.

4. Doris Weatherford. *A History of the American Suffrage Movement.* New York: MTM, 2005. Print. 227.

5. Ibid. 228.

6. Ibid. 242.

7. Jacqueline Van Voris. *Carrie Chapman Catt: A Public Life.* New York: Feminist, 1987. Print. 160.

8. Elizabeth C. Stanton et al., *History of Woman Suffrage.* New York: Fowler & Wells, 1881. Print. 624.

Chapter 9. The Legacy of Suffrage

1. Ruth Barnes Moynihan. *Second to None: A Documentary History of American Women, Volume II: From 1865 to the Present.* Lincoln, NE: University of Nebraska Press, 1993. Print. 322.

2. Ibid. 324.

3. Doris Weatherford. *A History of the American Suffrage Movement.* New York: MTM, 2005. Print. 143-144.

4. G.J. Barker-Benfield and Catherine Clinton. *Portraits of American Women From Settlement to the Present.* New York: Oxford UP, 1998. Print. 445-446.

5. Jeff Hill. *Defining Moments: Woman's Suffrage.* Detroit: Omnigraphics, 2006. Print. 91.

6. Gail Collins. *America's Women: 400 Years of Dolls, Drudges, Helpmates, and Heroines.* New York: Harpercollins, 2003. Print. 450.

INDEX

abolition, 28–33, 37, 39,
41–43, 47–49, 51
Adams, Abigail, 19–20
Adams, John, 19–20
Addams, Jane, 67
amendments,
Equal Rights, 90–91
Fifteenth, 50–53, 59
Fourteenth, 48, 49, 59
Nineteenth, 73, 74, 78–80,
83–86, 88, 90
Sixteenth, 72
American Equal Rights
Association, 49
American Woman Suffrage
Association, 52–53, 56–57,
61, 64
Anthony, Susan B., 8, 33, 42,
43, 44, 49, 51, 52–53, 57,
59, 60, 63

Blackwell, Henry, 37, 49, 51
Blatch, Harriet Stanton, 67, 68
Bloomer, Amelia, 33
bloomers, 33
Bonds of Womanhood, The, 27
Burn, Harry, 84

Catt, Carrie Chapman, 63, 72,
83
Civil War, 47, 72
Committee on Woman
Suffrage, 73
Condit, John, 22
Congressional Union, 71, 72,
74

Douglass, Frederick, 47, 48

Field, Sara Bard, 73
First National Women's Rights
Convention, 38–39

Gage, Matilda Joslin, 8
Greeley, Horace, 36, 50
Grimké, Angelina, 28
Grimké, Sarah, 28

Harper, Ida Huston, 8
History of Woman Suffrage, A, 8

Industrial Revolution, 64

Kelley, Abbey, 30

Maria, Or the Wrongs of Woman, 23
M'Clintock, Mary Ann, 7, 13
Milholland, Inez, 71
Mott, Lucretia, 7, 10, 13,
30–31

National American Woman
Suffrage Association, 61,
63–64, 69, 72, 76, 79, 80,
82, 84, 89
National Association Opposed
to Woman Suffrage, 63
National Woman's Party, 74,
79, 81, 84
National Woman's Suffrage
Association, 52, 53, 57, 61
National Women's Christian
Temperance Union, 62

Oberlin College, 37, 42
Ohio Constitutional
  Convention, 38

Pankhurst, Emmeline, 68
Parkman, Francis, 32
Paul, Alice, 68–71, 73–76, 90
Pierce, Charlotte Woodward,
  14, 79

Quakers, 20, 28

Rankin, Jeanette, 84
religion, 17, 18, 19, 20, 26–27,
  93
Revolution, 52, 57
Rochester Convention, 31–33

Salem Convention, 37–38
Second Great Awakening,
  26–27
Self–Supporting Women,
  Equality League of, 68
Seneca Falls Convention, 6, 7,
  9–14, 31, 32, 33, 36, 79
Sentiments, Declaration of,
  9–10, 13, 14
Shaw, Anna Howard, 63, 82
Stanton, Elizabeth Cady, 7–11,
  30–32, 33, 42, 43, 44, 48,
  49, 51–53, 57, 63, 67, 93–94
Steinem, Gloria, 91
Stone, Lucy, 33, 37, 49, 51,
  52, 63
Supreme Court, US, 59, 60, 91

temperance, 28, 33, 42, 43, 62
Thoughts on the Education of Daughters,
  23
Tracy, Hannah, 42
Train, George Francis, 51, 52
Truth, Sojourner, 39–44

Vindication of the Rights of Women, A,
  20, 23

Washington DC march, 70, 71
Wesleyan Chapel, 7, 11
Willard, Frances, 62
Wilson, Woodrow, 73, 74,
  78–80
Wollstonecraft, Mary, 20–22,
  23
Woman's Journal, 57, 64
Women Voters, League of, 80,
  89
Women's Trade Union League,
  64
Woodhull, Victoria, 58, 92
World Anti–Slavery
  Convention, 30–31
World War I, 72, 74
Wright, Martha Coffin, 7
Wyoming Territory, 58

ABOUT THE AUTHOR

Marcia Amidon Lusted is the author of more than 50 books for young readers, as well as hundreds of magazine articles. She is an assistant editor for Cobblestone Publishing, a writing instructor, and a musician. She lives in New Hampshire with her family.

PHOTO CREDITS